D1567538

ANNE GARDON

THE GOURMET'S GARDEN

COOKING WITH EDIBLE FLOWERS, HERBS AND BERRIES

Green Frog Publishing

Contents

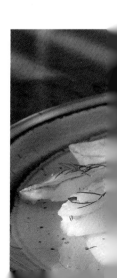

Foreword

I love gardening just as much as I love cooking. So imagine my joy when I take a stroll in the garden, basket in hand, to pick flowers, herbs and berries to make up a feast.

I call my brand of cooking C.H.E.F.'s cuisine — cheap, healthy, easy and fast. Though I enjoy preparing gourmet meals, I don't like slaving over a hot stove while my guests are enjoying themselves in the next room. And I'd rather read a good book than spend hours candying lackluster flowers to decorate my cakes.

I cook for fun, not to impress.

So, no fancy presentation, no long and involved recipes in this book, only easy-to-prepare dishes with ideas for making them your own, as well as personal gardening tips.

Bon appétit,

Anne Gardon

INTRODUCTION
The gourmet's garden

Nasturtium

My garden is like my cooking — exuberant, colorful, spontaneous, a little wild but very tasty.

In my garden, herbs, edible flowers and berries are not banished to the vegetable patch, but grow among ornamental plants and shrubs.

Tarragon makes a lush foreground to black-eyed Susans. Honeysuckle climbs the front porch, attracting hummingbirds. Beebalm, another favorite food of these tiny birds, shares a shady spot with daylilies. Marigold and nasturtiums add color to vegetable beds while protecting plants from pests.

FLOWERS GALORE!
Flowers make a pretty garnish for a dish. Unfortunately, most edible flowers — and there are hundreds — have about as much taste as iceberg lettuce.

Only a few have real culinary potential.

Nasturtium (*photo above*): the whole plant (stems, leaves, flowers and unripened fruit) has a sharp peppery taste. Add leaves to salads, sprinkle petals on pasta and rice dishes. Flower buds and green fruit can be pickled and used instead of capers.

Chives: flowers and sprigs have a mild onion flavor. Delicious in mashed potatoes, salads, sandwiches, with eggs and just about any dish that calls for onions.

Beebalm: hummingbirds love it and so do I. Fresh or dried, the leaves make a fragrant herbal tea. The flowers have a powerful, spicy, almost minty taste that goes equally well with meat dishes and desserts.

Calendula: ranging from bright orange to pale yellow, calendula petals — fresh or frozen — are used mostly for garnishing salads, soups and desserts. When dried, they lose their slight tangy taste, but dried petals make an inexpensive saffron substitute for coloring rice.

Marigold: I only grow miniature marigolds, *Tagetes tenuifolia* (Tangerine Gem, Lemon Gem, Lulu), milder in taste than the large variety. The dainty star-like blooms have a citrus flavor and literally cover the compact plants. Grown in the vegetable garden, marigolds are beneficial to potatoes, tomatoes and beans.

Daylily: it grows along country roads and a multitude of cultivars bloom in ornamental gardens. Some are bitter or may be toxic. Though I have only found one reference to toxic daylilies in all the literature on edible flowers, I limit my use to the safe orange variety that has naturalized in the wild.

Let's not forget **vegetable and herb flowers**. Basil flowers have the same taste as the leaves but are sweeter.

Opposite: Pineapple sage

Coriander and arugula flowers are delicious in salads. So are broccoli flowers. Once the broccoli head is harvested, let the side florets bloom. Rosemary and pineapple sage bloom indoors in January and February and bring a welcome touch of color to winter fare.

Popular in the south of France and Italy, squash blossoms are certainly the best-known edible flowers. And some cultivars have been especially created to produce huge flowers with thick petals. While all squash blossoms are edible, only male flowers should be picked as the female flower produces the fruit. How do you tell them apart? Just look inside. The male flower's sex organ appropriately resembles a penis, while that of the female flower resembles a crown.

Candied flowers

Though I am not in the habit of candying flowers, I have mastered the technique. Here is how to proceed.

Beat one egg white with a fork until just cloudy. Using a small brush, thoroughly coat flower petals — pansies, rose, borage, dianthus, honeysuckle — with egg white and sprinkle with granulated sugar (do not use confectioner's sugar as it gives them a dull finish). Let dry on a rack, in a warm, dry place. Store in an airtight container for up to a week.

Honeysuckle

Flower butters

Beebalm, nasturtium, chive and scented geranium preserve all their flavor when combined with butter. Mince petals and leaves and mix with soft butter. Shape into a log or drop spoonfuls onto a cookie sheet, and freeze. Store in freezer bags. Use to flavor desserts and as cake frosting or spread.

Freezing

Chive florets, beebalm and calendula petals freeze well. Spread on a cookie sheet, freeze, then store in a rigid container. Use to garnish or add flavor to dishes.

FLOWER SELECTION

It is important to use flowers that have not been treated with pesticides or other chemicals — flowers from your garden or a gourmet store, NOT the florist.

Here is a partial list of edible flowers:

Anise hyssop (agastache)
Annual sweet pea
Apple blossoms
Bachelor's buttons (centaurea, a.k.a cornflower)
Beebalm
Borage
Calendula
Camomile
Chives
Chrysanthemum
Dandelion
Daylily
Dianthus and pinks
Elderberry
Feverfew matricaria
Geranium
Gladiolus
Hibiscus
Honeysuckle
Hosta
Lavatera
Lavender
Marigold
Nasturtium
Ox-eye daisy
Pansy and violet
Rose
Sunflower
Tulip
Yarrow

Anise hyssop is one of my favorite herbs. The leaves and baby blue flowers have a sweet licorice taste and go well in salads, seafood dishes and desserts. Flower tops steeped in vodka (4-5 clusters for 500 ml) for about a week give the alcohol a "pastis" taste. Served with water and ice or mixed with fruit juice, anise hyssop alcohol makes a delicious drink.

Feverfew is another favorite of mine. A biennial, it blooms all summer long and reseeds itself without becoming invasive. It grows equally well in sun or partial shade, tolerates most types of soil and protects other plants from bugs. As a spray, feverfew tea is a powerful insect repellent.

In the kitchen, use feverfew sparingly as the taste is quite strong. Leaves and flowers can be sprinkled on salads and added to vinaigrettes for flavor. Dried flowers make a fragrant herbal tea that is said to help relieve migraine headaches.

Feverfew

TOXIC FLOWERS

It is useful to know what flowers are edible, but imperative to know which ones are toxic!

Here is a partial list of toxic plants, some of which are extremely dangerous.

Anemone
Autumn Crocus (Colchicum autumnale)
Bleeding heart
Buttercup
Daffodil
Delphinium (Larkspur)
Foxglove (Digitalis)
Hydrangea
Iris
Lily-of-the-valley
Lupine
Monkshood (Aconitum)
Perennial sweet pea
Poinsettia
Rhododendron and azalea
Wisteria

AROMATIC HERBS

I was born in Provence, the land of thyme and lavender. So it is no surprise that aromatic herbs take top billing in my cooking, and growing my own allows me to experiment with a whole new range of scents and flavors. My lemon basil apple sauce, lovage pot-au-feu and lamb with lemon verbena were created through much testing and tasting.

Herbs have three powerful arguments in their favor. They are easy to grow, they protect other plants from bugs and some are quite ornamental.

Here are the herbs growing in my garden:

Basil
Coriander
Dill
Horseradish
Lovage
Mint
Summer savory
Tarragon
Thyme

I grow tender perennials such as marjoram, rosemary, bay leaf, sage, oregano, scented geranium and lemon verbena, in containers that I bring indoors in the fall and keep in a bright, cool (50-60 °F/10-15 °C) room.

Preserving herbs

Freeze tarragon, lovage, scented geranium and lemon verbena leaves in air-tight freezer bags (I freeze herbs raw, without blanching). Tarragon is best picked in spring when tender. Remove tough branches and freeze leaves. Lovage, scented geranium and lemon verbena leaves can be harvested throughout the growing season.

Mint, lemon balm and beebalm can be preserved in ice when used for herbal tea. Fill ice cube trays halfway with chopped leaves or blossoms, cover with water and freeze. Unmold and store in sealed freezer bags. The sweet flavor of basil is best preserved in pesto (page 54).

Savory butters can be made like flower butters. Tarragon and dill butters are especially well suited to fish and poultry dishes. Mint butter goes well with lamb.

Rosemary, marjoram, thyme, savory and sage dry without losing their flavor. Cinnamon basil, lemon basil, lemon verbena, mint and beebalm can also be dried for herbal teas.

Lovage, coriander and dill seeds can be picked when green, and frozen. They are great in salad dressings and bean dishes.

Harvest dry seeds at the end of the season for culinary use and for reseeding the following year.

Drying

To dry herbs, spread on a fine mesh (mosquito net stretched over a frame is ideal) or place in paper bags. Use paper bags for herbs with little water content such as thyme, rosemary or savory. The soft leaves of beebalm, basil or mint will often get moldy in a bag before drying. Dry herbs in a warm, dry place then store in airtight containers or glass jars. Never expose to sun either when drying or storing.

Dried herbs can be blended to create complex flavors. Here are some ideas:

- rosemary, marjoram, thyme, summer savory, oregano for tomato-based sauces, pizza and Italian dishes,
- dill seeds, lemon basil and lemon thyme for poultry and seafood,
- dried lovage seeds crushed with sea salt to replace celery salt.

A bunch of aromatic herbs

Red currants

BERRIES
Strawberries

I do not grow strawberries because it is too much trouble, and berry producers abound in my area. I do not freeze whole strawberries either, as they become grey and mushy when defrosted and lose their flavor. My preferred freezing method is in a coulis, that is, puréed with sugar in the blender or food processor. Other than that, I gorge myself with strawberries while they are in season and after that am quite content to wait until next year's season comes around.

Raspberries

Strawberries only come in red, but raspberries can also be yellow, orange or even black. The latter, not to be confused with blackberries, are rarely cultivated but grow wild in unattended fields. They contain more seeds than the red raspberry, so I use them mainly for fruit juices, syrups and jellies.

Raspberries freeze well, preserving all their flavor and color. Spread on a cookie sheet, freeze, then store in a rigid container.

Currants and gooseberries

Currants come in red, yellow and black. The fruit are small and grow in clusters. Red currants (and yellow) have a tangy taste and make a great base for herb jellies. Black currant is used to make syrup and a liqueur.

Gooseberries have bigger, sweeter fruit, first green then purple when ripe. Great in pies, they are even better in sauces for meat and venison.

Currant bushes make a pretty hedge for my vegetable garden while providing food for birds and small animals.

Blueberries

Two kinds of blueberry plants grow in my area. The creeping blueberry I transplanted in my shade garden blooms with enthusiasm in spring, without ever producing fruit but making a lovely ground cover. The tall variety would normally yield fruit but I have pruned it like a bonsai, so I have to rely on wild or store-bought blueberries for pies and jams.

Blueberries go well with pork and venison. They freeze well using the same method as for raspberries.

WEIGHTS AND MEASURES

Logically, dry ingredients — flour, sugar, even vegetables — should be measured by weight, either in grams or ounces. But not everyone has a kitchen scale. Liquids should be measured by volume (ml, fluid ounces). How complicated! It's so much easier to use cups and spoons.

Bearing that in mind, I have marked all measures by volume, except in some instances for meat or cheese, when it is handy to know the weight for the sake of purchasing.
Here is the conversion chart, with figures rounded up or down for easier measuring.

1 tsp. = 5 ml

1 tbsp. = 15 ml

1 cup = 250 ml = 8 fluid ounces

4 cups = 1 liter = 1 quart

1 gallon = 4 liters = 4 quarts

Sunflower buds in vinaigrette

Sunflowers provide us with seeds to munch on and oil for cooking. But did you know that the flower buds are edible too?

Crunchy, meaty, with a slight taste of artichoke heart, the buds are great as appetizers or a side dish. Bitter when raw, they must be cooked with two or three changes of water to remove the bitterness.

Pick buds growing on side branches when they reach the size of an apricot. Removing the lower flowers will increase the size of the remaining sunflower.

Prepare this dish at the last minute, as the buds turn a strange fluorescent green when cooling.

INGREDIENTS

12 sunflower buds

2 tbsp. (30 ml) lemon juice

1 tbsp. (15 ml) mustard

1/4 cup (65 ml) olive oil

Salt, pepper

Bring a pot of water to a boil and blanch sunflower buds for 2 minutes. Drain. Add more water, bring to a boil, blanch another 2 minutes. Drain and repeat a third time if still bitter.

Mix lemon juice and mustard. Beat in oil, add salt and pepper to taste.

Toss buds with vinaigrette. Serve immediately.

You may also serve the buds with Gribiche sauce (page 88).

SERVES 2-4.

Yogurt cheese with yarrow

Choose a natural yogurt or, better, make your own, as some commercial yogurts with added thickening agents will not drain adequately. Goat's milk yogurt will not give satisfactory results either.

Do not throw away the drained liquid. Rich in minerals, it can be added to soups or make a refreshing drink.

Pick yarrow early or late in the day, when the air is cool.

INGREDIENTS

2 cups (500 ml) plain yogurt

2 tbsp. (30 ml) chopped yarrow flowers

1 tsp. (15 ml) salt

Pepper to taste

Combine all ingredients. Pour into a jelly bag or a colander lined with cheesecloth. Let drain 12 hours in the fridge.

Serve cold.

This fragrant fresh cheese is ideal as an appetizer or in sandwiches.

MAKES 1 CUP (250 ML).

Variation: Use a strong herb such as thyme, rosemary or summer savory instead of yarrow.

Yarrow

Yarrow's generic name, *Achillea millefolium*, refers to Achilles, the legendary hero of the Trojan War. He reportedly used the plant to treat his wounded soldiers. Yarrow indeed has many healing properties. It can be used externally to treat minor wounds or internally as a tonic for the heart and circulatory system. For centuries, women have used yarrow tea to relieve heavy menstrual periods.

Whenever I get a bruise, a burn or an insect bite, I collect a handful of yarrow leaves, crush them in a mortar or in my hand with a few drops of water and apply the poultice to the wound. I get relief within minutes.

Flowers and leaves have a strong

peppery taste. Use them sparingly in salads and vinaigrettes. Don't take large doses of yarrow or use for long periods of time — no more than three times a week — as several of its 120 chemical compounds are toxic and may provoke headaches and dizzy spells.

A drought-resistant and easy-care perennial, yarrow grows best in light, well-drained soil and in full sun. New cultivars have been created in shades of red and yellow, and these have an important place in my garden. But for cooking, I only use wild yarrow. I have transplanted a couple of plants in my vegetable plot where they attract beneficial insects. The leaves make a good compost activator and a powerful liquid fertilizer.

Steep yarrow leaves in water for a couple of weeks. Drain and dilute 1:10. Water or spray the plants with the solution.

Other plants can be added to this liquid fertilizer for a richer brew, such as comfrey, dandelion (leaves and roots), stinging nettle, tansy, plantain, thistle — all those weeds you thought were useless.

Cheese balls with chives

INGREDIENTS

1/2 lb (250 g) cream cheese

12 chive flower heads

1/2 cup (125 ml) chive stalks, chopped

Place cheese in the freezer for about 10 minutes to harden.

Pull florets off the flower heads. Reserve stalks.

With wet hands, make a dozen cheese balls. Roll half in chive florets and half in chopped stalks. Pick a segment of stalk in each ball for easy handling and serve cold.

MAKES ABOUT 12 CHEESE BALLS.

Flower and herb fritters

Serve these savory fritters as an appetizer or as part of a buffet al fresco.

BATTER:

1 egg, separated

1 tbsp. (15 ml) flour

1/4 cup (65 ml) water or beer

Salt, pepper

Oil for deep frying

1 cup (250 ml) mixed flowers: calendula, chive, squash blossom, daylily, hosta

1 cup (250 ml) mixed herbs: basil, mint and lemon balm leaves, tarragon sprigs

Beat egg white until stiff, add yolk and beat some more.

Sprinkle with flour and beat while slowly adding water or beer. Season to taste.

Clean flowers and herbs, preferably without using water, to avoid spluttering while frying.

Dip flowers and herbs in batter and deep fry until golden. Make small batches as the fritters cook in a few seconds.

Serve immediately.

SERVES 6-8.

Chives
Clumps of chives decorate almost every flowerbed in my garden, but look their very best in the rock garden. In May and June, the nectar-rich flowers attract bees, swallowtail butterflies and a multitude of other insects. They share their long blooming season with irises, peonies and clematis.

Cheese balls with chives

A member of the garlic family, chives grow best in full sun but tolerate shade. Rich soil is better but poor soil will do. In other words, chives grow in all but the most extreme conditions. A hardy perennial, it will reseed itself without becoming invasive.

Stalks and flowers have a mild onion taste that goes well with egg dishes and in vinaigrettes. Sprinkle florets on green salad and cold soups, add to sandwiches and pasta dishes.

Feta and herb pinwheels

I always keep some puff pastry in my freezer. Easy to use and versatile, with a fine taste and texture, ready-made puff pastry can be used in many ways, from the classic millefeuille *to these pinwheels bursting with flavor. The dough handles better when chilled.*

INGREDIENTS

1/4 lb (100 g) feta cheese, creamy if possible

1 tbsp. (15 ml) olive oil

3 tbsp. (45 ml) mixed fresh herbs, finely chopped: thyme, rosemary, summer savory, marjoram, chives
or:
2 tbsp. (30 ml) pesto (see page 54)

Salt, pepper

1 package (14 oz/396 g) puff pastry

Preheat the oven to 400 °F (200 °C).

Crush the feta with a fork and combine with oil and herbs. Season with salt, if necessary, and pepper.

One package of puff pastry contains 2 blocks of dough. Roll out each block into a rectangle 6 x 10 inches (15 x 25 cm).

Spread half of the cheese mixture on each rectangle and roll into a log 6 inches (15 cm) long. Cut into slices 1 inch (2 cm) thick, flatten the slices with a spatula and place on a non-stick cookie sheet. Repeat with second log.

Bake 10 minutes, flip over and bake another 10 minutes until golden. Serve warm.

MAKES 12 PINWHEELS.

Variation: Use a creamy goat cheese or a blue cheese.

Herb and ricotta filo nests

Filo pastry is just as versatile and easy to use as puff pastry, in sweet and savory dishes alike. Once opened, the package may be frozen and defrosted again a couple of times, before the sheets of very thin pastry will start to dry up.

INGREDIENTS

2 cups (450 g) creamy ricotta cheese

1/4 cup (65 ml) mixed fresh herbs, finely chopped: basil, mint, tarragon, lemon balm, marjoram

Salt, pepper

2 sheets of filo pastry

Olive oil

1 tsp. (5 ml) mixed dried herbs

Combine ricotta, herbs, salt and pepper to taste and mix well. Reserve.

Preheat the oven to 375 °F (190 °C).

Spread one filo sheet, brush with olive oil and sprinkle with dried herbs. Cover with the second sheet and cut crosswise to get 4 squares.

Place squares into muffin tins and bake 10-15 minutes or until golden. Cool.

Fill nests with cheese mixture. Drizzle with olive oil and serve.

SERVES 4.

Variation: Add 2 tbsp. (30 ml) chive florets to the cheese.

Tzatziki

This refreshing appetizer is ideal for a picnic.

INGREDIENTS

1 seedless cucumber

1 tbsp. (15 ml) salt

1 cup (250 ml) plain yogurt

15 mint leaves, finely chopped

10 chive sprigs, finely chopped

1 garlic clove

Pepper

Peel cucumber and cut into thin slices. Place in a colander and toss with salt. Let drain 1 hour.

Rinse under cold running water. Drain and pat dry.

Mince or crush garlic with a garlic press. Combine all ingredients. Season to taste and chill at least one hour before serving.

Mint

The British cook mint with lamb, the French add it to peas. The Arabs make it into a tea, served scalding hot, and gardeners love to crush a few leaves while going about their chores.

   Various types of mint grow in my garden — peppermint, orange mint, chocolate — among daylilies which control their wild exuberance. I use fresh leaves in lemonades and salads, to flavor meat dishes and chocolate desserts.

   Mint can be dried or frozen. To freeze, fill ice cube trays halfway with chopped leaves, top with water and freeze. Unmold and keep in a sealed freezer bag. To make tea or lemonade, just drop one or more ice cubes into hot water.

   All mints are stimulating, helpful to the digestion, and antiseptic.

Mint spring rolls

Light yet nourishing, these rolls are the perfect finger food for an al fresco *party.*

INGREDIENTS

2/3 lb (300 g) chicken fillet or breast

2 tbsp. (30 ml) light soy sauce

2 tbsp. (30 ml) sesame oil

1 tbsp. (15 ml) minced fresh ginger

2 oz (100 g) rice vermicelli

1/2 seedless cucumber

3 green onions

12 mint leaves

12 rice pancakes 6 inches (15 cm) wide

Salt, pepper

Cooking oil

Cut chicken into 12 thin strips. Combine soy sauce, sesame oil and ginger. Toss chicken with sauce and let stand while preparing the other ingredients.

Crush vermicelli coarsely with your hands and cover with boiling water. Let stand 10 minutes until soft. Drain, rinse under cold running water, drain again, and toss with a few drops of sesame oil to prevent noodles from sticking.

Peel cucumber and cut into 12 sticks, 4 inches (10 cm) long. Cut green onions in 4 inches (10 cm) segments then in half lengthwise.

Heat some oil in a non-stick frying pan and stir-fry chicken, 2 minutes. Remove pan from heat, cover and let stand until the chicken has cooled.

Soften rice pancakes in a large bowl of tepid water, three at a time. Spread on a clean dishcloth.

Fill pancakes one at a time, keeping remaining pancakes covered with damp cloth. Place 1 chicken strip in the center with a cucumber stick, green onions, vermicelli and a mint leaf. Fold ends over the filling and roll up tight, taking care not to tear the thin wrapper. Cut in half. Repeat with remaining ingredients.

Serve with a soy dip (see Thai salad, page 64)

MAKES 12 ROLLS OR 24 PIECES.

Stuffed daylilies

Daylilies are among my favorite perennials. Easy to care for, they have a lush foliage, bloom abundantly even if each flower lasts only one day — hence their name —, and most of all, they are edible.

INGREDIENTS

1 cup (250 ml) creamy goat cheese

1 egg yolk

1 cup (250 ml) chopped greens (watercress, spinach, arugula)

1 tbsp. (15 ml) fresh basil or tarragon, chopped

Salt, pepper

12 daylily flowers

12 chive stalks

1 tbsp. (15 ml) olive oil

Mix together cheese, egg yolk, greens and herbs. Season to taste.

Dip chive stalks in hot water to make them more flexible.

Cut the green tip off each flower and pull out the stamens and pistils. Fill cup with cheese mixture and tie with a chive stalk.

Heat some oil in a non-stick frying pan. Fry stuffed flowers, 5 to 6 seconds each side to wilt the petals. Serve immediately.

The same cheese mixture can be used to stuff squash blossoms.

SERVES 4.

Daylily roots and shoots

The tuber-like roots and young shoots of daylilies are edible. The tubers have a yellow skin and white crunchy meat, similar to radish. The light green shoots have a crisp peppery taste and are superb raw in salads.

But digging up and cleaning daylily roots and shoots is a long and painstaking task. What you see in the photograph took me close to one hour to harvest and another hour to clean. And though I prepared a stunning appetizer with the harvest, never again will I go to that much trouble. I am quite content to just eat the flowers.

*Gougère is a savory choux pastry flavored with
cheese. In Burgundy, gougères are traditionally
served with wine-tasting in cellars.*

Herb gougères

INGREDIENTS

1/4 cup (65 ml) butter

1 cup (250 ml) water

1/2 tsp. (2.5 ml) salt

1 cup (250 ml) flour

4 eggs

1/2 cup (125 ml) chopped fresh herbs (tarragon, basil, chives, marjoram)

1/2 cup (125 ml) grated strong cheddar or gruyère cheese

1 egg, beaten

Preheat the oven to 375 °F (190 °C). In a heavy saucepan, combine butter, water, salt and bring to a boil.

Add flour all at once and stir with a wooden spoon over low heat until the mixture leaves the sides of the pan and forms a ball, about 1 minute. Remove from heat and beat in eggs, one at a time, until a smooth dough is obtained. To make this easier, use an electric mixer.

Add herbs and cheese. Mix well.

Drop batter by teaspoonfuls onto greased baking sheets — or use a pastry bag — leaving about 2 inches (5 cm) between each puff. Brush top with beaten egg for a shiny finish and bake for 35 to 40 minutes, until golden.

With a sharp knife, make a small hole in each gougère to let trapped steam escape, then let stand in the turned-off oven with the door open, until firm. If you remove the gougères too quickly, they will collapse.

Serve as finger food, appetizers, or with a salad or a soup.

MAKES 12 TO 18 GOUGÈRES.

Variations: Bake the gougère in a ring shape and fill the center with grilled vegetables. Or stuff with a savory filling.

Goat cheese medallions with basil

Choose a firm cheese. It will not fall apart during cooking.

INGREDIENTS

1 goat cheese log

1/2 cup (125 ml) dry bread crumbs

Olive oil

2 large ripe but still firm tomatoes

Salt, pepper

12 chopped basil leaves

Cut cheese log into 12 slices, removing ends. Flatten slices with a spatula or the palms of your hands and roll in bread crumbs.

Heat 2 tbsp. oil (30 ml) in a non-stick pan and fry cheese slices, a few seconds on each side, until golden.

Cut tomatoes in thick slices, keeping the four largest. Set aside the rest for later use. Arrange tomato slices on serving plates, top with cheese, sprinkle with basil and drizzle with olive oil.

Serve immediately.

SERVES 4.

Cold avocado and coriander soup

Make this smooth and refreshing soup at the last minute to prevent the avocado from darkening.

INGREDIENTS

2 ripe avocados

juice and grated peel of 1 lime

1 cup (250 ml) coriander leaves

1 cup (250 ml) buttermilk or plain yogourt

1 small chili pepper, seeded*

2 cups (500 ml) water

Salt, pepper

Combine all ingredients (except salt and pepper) in the blender and process at high speed until creamy. Season to taste. Chill before serving.

I like mine really thick and creamy but you can add more water to suit your taste.

SERVES 4.

* *Wear gloves to seed pepper.*

Cream of borage

Warning: pregnant or nursing women should avoid borage as it may stimulate milk flow.

Borage leaves have a cool cucumber taste. But they are also quite hairy and rather unpalatable when raw. At least for me! But I still want the purifying benefits of the plant — wonderful for the complexion — so I prepare this soup in the same way as the cold avocado-coriander soup.

I replace the avocados with a cup of raw chopped leaves and a cucumber, peeled and seeded, then strain the soup after processing to remove lumps.

Garnish with borage flowers and serve chilled.

SERVES 4.

Cold tarragon and zucchini soup

INGREDIENTS

1 tbsp. (15 ml) butter

1 tbsp. (15 ml) flour

2 cups (500 ml) milk

3 grated zucchini

1/3 cup (85 ml) chopped fresh tarragon

Salt, pepper

Melt butter in a heavy saucepan, sprinkle with flour and stir, one minute, over medium heat. Add milk, stir and bring slowly to a boil. Add grated zucchini and simmer 10 minutes. Season to taste.

Process in a blender until creamy. Chill.

Serve sprinkled with fresh tarragon.

SERVES 2.

Cold pea and mint soup

Mint enhances the sweetness of peas without overpowering their delicate flavor. This cold soup is perfect to bring on a picnic.

INGREDIENTS

1 1/2 (375 ml) cups water

1 tbsp. (15 ml) sugar

4 cups (1 liter) shelled peas, fresh or thawed

1/2 cup (125 ml) light cream or buttermilk

10 mint leaves

Salt, pepper

Combine water, sugar and salt. Bring to a boil and cook peas until tender. Cool.

Place peas and their cooking liquid, light cream and mint in a blender and process at high speed until smooth. Add more water if too thick. Strain if desired and chill.

SERVES 4.

Tom-lo-zuc

Funny name, right? But what better name for this delicate soup made with tomatoes, lovage and zucchini?

When I moved to the country a dozen years or so ago, I didn't know much about growing vegetables. So the first year, I planted four cherry-tomato plants and all the seeds in my zucchini seed-package. If you are a gardener, you know what happened. By September, I was submerged in cherry tomatoes and zucchini. Then I hit on the idea of combining them with lovage to make a soup. It has become one of my favorites.

A gardening tip: in my humble opinion, the best variety of cherry tomatoes is Sweet 100, as much for its exceptional flavor as its high yield. The tiny fruits are sweet as candy, and children just love them!

INGREDIENTS

4 cups (1 liter) cherry tomatoes

2 medium size zucchini, in chunks

2 stalks lovage

2 cups (500 ml) water

Salt, pepper

Olive oil

Combine tomatoes, zucchini, lovage and water in a large pot. Season to taste and bring to a boil. Reduce heat and simmer until zucchini is cooked, 15 to 20 minutes. Or cook 1 minute in a pressure cooker.

Press through a fine sieve or a food mill to remove tomato skins and seeds.

Season to taste and drizzle with olive oil. Serve warm or cold. Freezes well.

SERVES 4.

Herb gazpacho

The word "gazpacho" comes from the Arabic and means soaked bread. Authentic Spanish gazpacho is thickened with soft breadcrumbs, but personally, I prefer to use gelatin. The result is an eye-catching gazpacho, smooth yet crunchy.

The choice of vegetables depends on your taste buds and whatever your garden can provide.

INGREDIENTS

1 tbsp. (15 ml/1 packet) unflavored gelatin

1/2 cup (125 ml) cold water

2 cups (500 ml) tomato or vegetable juice

1 cucumber

4-5 radishes

1 stalk celery

1 cup (250 ml) mixed fresh herbs, chopped: parsley, coriander, basil, chives, lemon balm, mint

1 garlic clove

1 small chili pepper, seeded*

Juice of 1 lemon

1/4 cup (65 ml) olive oil

Salt, pepper

In a small saucepan, sprinkle gelatin over water and soften. Then place over low heat and stir until gelatin has dissolved. Or microwave 1 minute at maximum. Stir in tomato juice and chill one hour to set.

Mince vegetables and herbs. You may use a food processor fitted with metal blades. Combine with tomato juice, lemon juice and olive oil. Stir until well mixed. Season to taste.

Drizzle with olive oil and serve chilled, with lemon wedges.

SERVES 4-6.

* *Wear gloves to seed pepper.*

Savory and white bean soup

Just as flavorful dried as fresh, summer savory plays an important role in winter cooking. Perfect for seasoning grilled meats, in stuffings and simmered dishes, summer savory enhances the subtle flavor of white beans in this creamy soup, while reducing flatulence.

INGREDIENTS

1 tbsp. (15 ml) olive oil

1 onion, minced

2 cups (500 ml) chicken stock

1 can (19 oz/540 ml) white beans, drained and rinsed

2 tbsp. (30 ml) fresh summer savory or 1 tbsp. (15 ml) dried

Salt, pepper

Croutons

In a heavy saucepan, heat oil and cook onion until soft, about 1 minute.

Add chicken stock, white beans and summer savory. Season to taste. Bring to a boil, then simmer 5 minutes.

Process in a blender until smooth. Serve piping hot with croutons sautéed in olive oil or with Herb gougères (page 31).

SERVES 2-3.

Summer savory

Known since ancient times and grown in Charlemagne's gardens, savory is a Mediterranean herb with a strong, spicy flavor, reminiscent of thyme, camphor and mint. It is one of the hundred herbs used to make Chartreuse liqueur.

Stimulating, and some say aphrodisiac, summer savory helps reduce flatulence and is a must in bean dishes.

There are two types of savory. Summer savory is an annual. Winter savory is a tender perennial with a stronger aroma and tougher leaves. For decoration, I also grow a creeping savory, but for cooking I only use summer savory.

Garlic broth

Ready in a jiffy, this rich-flavored broth works wonders for colds. For extra strength, double the amount of garlic.

INGREDIENTS

2 tbsp. (30 ml) olive oil

2 minced garlic cloves

3 cups (750 ml) chicken stock

1/4 cup (65 ml) orzo*

1/4 cup (65 ml) grated cheese: Parmesan, gruyère or cheddar

Fresh marjoram or parsley, minced

* Orzo is rice-shaped pasta.
If unavailable, use cooked rice.

In a heavy saucepan, heat oil and cook garlic 30 seconds over medium heat.

Add chicken stock and bring to a boil. Add orzo and cook until tender, about 5 minutes.

Serve sprinkled with grated cheese and herbs.

SERVES 2-3.

Variation: Instead of orzo, ladle broth over toasted bread slices.

Garlic

You might say garlic played an important role in Napoleon's military setbacks. The Emperor was on the verge of crushing the Austrian army when he was seized with violent stomach cramps. Convinced he had been poisoned, he stopped on his way to Bohemia, giving his enemies ample time to regroup and later crush him at Waterloo. The alleged poisoning was actually a case of indigestion caused by a garlic-studded stew.

Common garlic has been cultivated for so long that it is difficult to know for sure what country it comes from. Babylonians made great use of it in cooking while Egyptians used garlic as a currency — a healthy slave was worth fifteen pounds of garlic. The Vikings took it with them on their long sea journeys and during World War II, Russian soldiers spread garlic paste on their wounds to prevent infection.

Garlic is antiseptic, stimulating, diuretic and purgative, and reduces blood pressure. Its active properties and pungent odor result from a volatile, sulphurated essential oil called allicin, rich in vitamins, minerals and enzymes.

Raw or cooked, garlic is an indispensable ingredient of Mediterranean and Asian cooking. Its strong smell blooms when garlic is crushed or minced, but mellows when cooked. Removing the sprout inside will further reduce odor and taste.

Garlic goes well with lamb, snails and seafood, stews and sauces (pesto, aioli). It enhances the flavor of salads, oils and vinegars. In Provence, chicken is roasted with 40 garlic cloves, which are then mashed and spread on toast.

Garlic grows well in rich, well-drained soil and a sunny location. Plant in fall or spring around rose bushes for pest control but do not plant close to beans or peas.

Daylily bud stir-fry

In China, daylilies (Hemerocallis fulva) are commonly used in soups and stews and represent an important food crop in the North. I have tested both dried and frozen daylily buds but was not impressed with the results. They are definitely tastier when fresh. Pick plump buds ready to bloom.

INGREDIENTS

1 fresh piece ginger, cherry-size

1/4 cup (65 ml) soy sauce

1 tbsp. (15 ml) lemon juice

1/2 lb (250 g) chicken fillet or breast, cubed

1 medium onion

2 zucchini

24 daylily buds

Cooking oil

Mince or crush ginger with a garlic press. Combine with soy sauce and lemon. Toss chicken with mixture and reserve.

Slice onion into rings and zucchini into sticks.

In a wok or a skillet, heat 2 tbsp. (30 ml) oil and stir-fry onion, 1 minute. Remove with a slotted spoon. Stir-fry zucchini and reserve.

Add more oil. Drain chicken, reserving marinade. Stir-fry 2 minutes. Return vegetables to the pan with the daylily buds and the marinade. Cover and cook 3 minutes over medium heat.

Serve over a bed of Chinese noodles or rice.

Variation: Replace zucchini with snow peas, add mushrooms.

Calendula risotto

The essence of Italian country cooking, risotto is a rich creamy dish, full of flavor and aroma. A perfect setting for flowers, risotto can be garnished with ham or seafood, flavored with basil, tarragon or lovage — the combinations are infinite. But the rice should always be Italian short-grain rice such as Arborio.

INGREDIENTS

2 tbsp. (30 ml) butter

1 medium onion, minced

1 cup (250 ml) fresh mushrooms, sliced

3 + cups (750 ml +) chicken stock

1 1/2 cup (375 ml) Italian rice

1/2 cup (125 ml) calendula petals

Salt, pepper

Grated Parmesan

Melt butter in a large pot. Cook onion over medium heat until soft, about 1 minute. Add mushrooms and cook 3 minutes, stirring often.

Meanwhile, heat chicken stock separately.

Add rice to mushrooms and toss to coat with butter. Pour stock over*, add calendula petals, cover and simmer 20-25 minutes, until done. Add more stock during cooking if needed. Season to taste.

Serve sprinkled with Parmesan cheese and more calendula petals.

* This is a short-cut, I admit. The traditional recipe calls for adding the stock a little at a time and stirring until the liquid is completely absorbed before adding more. This method gives a special texture to the rice, creamy and crunchy at the same time. Adding the stock all at once makes for softer rice. Try both methods.

Calendula

Calendula, also known as pot marigold, has been used since ancient times as an inexpensive substitute for saffron. An annual, it grows well in rich, well-drained soil and reseeds itself profusely. Flower buds can be pickled like nasturtium buds and used in place of capers. I freeze petals — spread on a cookie sheet — to garnish soups and desserts. The bright orange of calendula petals brings sunshine to my plate during the dreary months of winter.

Nasturtium pizza

Nasturtium buds and flowers give a peppery taste to this pizza, garnished with other unusual ingredients such as goat cheese and zucchini slices. If this is really too weird for you, just add nasturtium to your regular pizza.

INGREDIENTS

1 pizza dough (20 in./50 cm wide)

1 cup (250 ml) spicy tomato sauce

1 small zucchini, thinly sliced

2 oz (100 g) goat or blue cheese

20 nasturtium buds and flowers

Olive oil

Preheat the oven to 375 °F (190 °C).

Roll out pizza dough, spread with tomato sauce, garnish with zucchini slices, crumbled cheese and nasturtiums. Drizzle with olive oil.

Bake for 30 minutes or until the sides are crisp.

Stuffed nasturtium flowers

Titillate your guests' taste buds with these tangy morsels.

INGREDIENTS

1 cup (250 ml) soft ricotta cheese

2 tbsp. (30 ml) olive oil

1 tbsp. (30 ml) fresh tarragon, minced

1 tsp. (5 ml) fresh chives, minced

Salt, pepper

12 nasturtium flowers

Combine cheese with oil and herbs, chill one hour. Stuff nasturtium flowers with the mixture using a pastry bag. Serve on melba toast or slices of cucumber for easy handling.

Nasturtiums

Gardeners and gourmets alike are fond of this pretty annual, easy to grow and delicious to eat. Its therapeutic properties are not to be overlooked either.

The species (*Tropaeolum majus*) comes from Peru and is a climbing plant, though compact cultivars have been developed. Rich in vitamin C and minerals, flowers and leaves have a tangy, mustardlike flavor much like watercress. Green buds and immature seeds can be pickled and used instead of capers or to flavor oils and vinegars. Leaves and flowers are great in salads and sandwiches. Minced, they can be incorporated into butters and soft cheeses.

You can also make a refreshing lemonade. In a blender, combine a couple of handfuls of leaves and flowers with 1 cup of water. Purée, add more water, lemon juice and sugar to taste. Mix well, strain and chill.

Nasturtiums stimulate appetite and help digestion.

Gardening

Nasturtiums are easy to grow, provided they have plenty of water during hot spells. Planted in poor soil, they will produce lots of flowers, while in rich soil they will produce mostly leaves. Wait after the last frost date to plant seeds, as they are sensitive to cold. For early blooms, start seeds indoors — use individual pots as nasturtium roots hate to be disturbed — 3-4 weeks before transplanting. In fall, harvest dried seeds for planting the following year and keep in a cool, dry place.

Nasturtiums play an important role in the vegetable garden. Planted with squash and tomatoes, they will keep bugs away. They are also beneficial to all members of the cabbage family, potatoes, radishes and apple trees. A spray can also be made with the leaves and used on these crops. Add a few drops of dishwashing liquid so the spray will adhere better. Strangely, while protecting other plants, nasturtiums are sometimes infested with aphids. It is a sign your soil has a lime deficiency. Dusting plants with lime will eliminate the problem.

Artichoke bottoms with tarragon sauce

Artichoke bottoms with tarragon sauce

To get twelve artichoke bottoms, you may need to purchase two or more cans (14 oz/398 ml) as the number of pieces varies from one brand to the other, and even from one can to the other. You can also use fresh artichokes when in season.

INGREDIENTS

1/4 cup (65 ml) butter

1 tbsp. (15 ml) flour

1 cup (250 ml) milk

Salt, pepper

1 tbsp. (15 ml) fresh tarragon, minced

2 tbsp. (30 ml) butter

2 cups (500 ml) mushrooms, sliced

12 artichoke bottoms

Melt butter in a small saucepan, sprinkle with flour and cook 1 minute over medium heat. Add milk and cook over medium heat until thick, stirring constantly.

Add tarragon, salt and pepper to taste and reserve.

In a skillet, melt 2 tbsp. (30 ml) butter and stir-fry mushrooms over medium-high heat until golden.

Place artichoke bottoms in an ovenproof dish. Fill artichoke centers with mushrooms. Season lightly and pour the béchamel sauce over.

Bake at 375 °F (190 °C) for 15 minutes to warm up artichokes then broil a few minutes until top is golden.

SERVES 4.

Variation: Replace mushrooms with cubed ham, chicken or a poached egg.

Fresh tarragon pasta

Making pasta is easy. You don't even need a pasta machine to roll out the dough as a rolling pin will do almost as well. Of course, a pasta machine is faster and may be a good investment if you like homemade pasta.

INGREDIENTS

2 cups (500 ml) flour

2 eggs

1 tsp. (5 ml) salt

3 tbsp. (45 ml) olive oil

1/4 cup (65 ml) fresh tarragon, minced

Cold water

In the bowl of a food processor, combine flour, eggs, salt, oil and tarragon. Add cold water — 1 tbsp. (15 ml) at a time — while processing by pulses until a smooth, elastic dough is formed. Add water while kneading. Chill one hour.

Roll out dough and cut into strips, 1/2 inch (1 cm) wide.

Bring a large pot of salted water to a boil. Throw in pasta and cook until tender, not more than 2 minutes. Drain and toss generously with olive oil or melted butter.

This pasta goes well with grilled shrimp.

SERVES 4.

Variations: Replace tarragon with other herbs; replace cold water with puréed vegetables (spinach, squash, tomato) for color.

Salt cod and potato salad with dill

This warm salad makes a nice light lunch or a nourishing first course.

INGREDIENTS

1 lb (500 g) salt cod

4 medium potatoes, peeled

1/2 cup (125 ml) olive oil

1/2 cup (125 ml) fresh dill, chopped

Salt, pepper

Soak cod in cold water overnight. Rinse under cold running water.

Bring a pot of water to a simmer and poach cod 5 minutes. Drain, cool slightly, then flake cod with a fork.

Cook potatoes in salted water until done but still firm. Drain, cool and cut into thick slices.

Heat half the oil in a skillet and fry potatoes on both sides until golden. Remove with a slotted spoon and arrange on serving plates. Season lightly.

Add remaining oil to the skillet and stir-fry cod 1 minute. Toss with dill and arrange over potatoes.

Serve warm.

Variation: Instead of salt cod, you may use hot smoked fish, like mackerel, Arctic char or salmon. Of course, do not soak overnight.

SERVES 3-4.

Dill

Used primarily to flavor pickled cucumbers, dill is an annual, native to the Mediterranean region and southern Russia. In ancient times, it was subject to a tax, like cumin, saffron and mint. Roman gladiators rubbed their bodies with dill essential oil and in the Middle Ages, dill was one of the herbs used in spells against witchcraft.

Dill goes well with potatoes, fish and in soups. Dried flowers make lovely, ethereal bouquets and seeds can be used to flavor herbal teas, marinades for meat or fish, vinegars and sauerkraut.

In the garden, dill is a good companion to all members of the cabbage family but inhibits the growth of carrots. An annual, it reseeds itself if left to go to seed.

Basil and beet flans

What a spectacular dish, and so easy to make too!

INGREDIENTS

1/2 cup (125 ml) beet greens
+ 16 whole leaves

1/2 lb (200 g) feta cheese

2 eggs, separated

1 cup (250 ml) basil leaves, chopped

2 medium beets, well cooked

1/2 cup (125 ml) light cream

Pepper

Olive oil

Preheat the oven to 375 °F (190 °C).

Steam beet greens. Reserve 16 whole leaves for lining molds and press remaining leaves to remove excess water.

Crumble feta cheese with a fork and mix with beet greens, egg yolks and 1/2 cup (125 ml) basil leaves. Or mix with a food processor.

Beat egg whites until stiff and fold into cheese mixture.

Brush 4 ramekin (custard) molds with olive oil and line with beet leaves, letting the excess hang over the edge. Fill with cheese-egg mixture. Fold leaves over.

Place molds in an ovenproof dish. Fill halfway with warm water.

Bake 30 minutes or until a skewer inserted in the center of a flan comes out clean.

Meanwhile, combine beets, cream and the remaining basil in a blender and purée until smooth. Strain through a fine sieve to remove lumps.

Ladle beet coulis onto serving plates, unmold flans in their center and serve.

SERVES 4.

Basil

There used to be just one type of basil, common or sweet basil with large, shiny leaves and the sweet smell of summer. Now, basil leaves can be purple, green or two-tone, smooth or ruffled, large or tiny. Flowers are mauve or pink, with some clusters the size of a fist. Seed companies list up to 15 different cultivars. Most are useless in the kitchen but lovely in the garden. Here are the ones I have tested over the years.

Cinnamon basil: a tall (1 1/2 ft/ 45 cm), elegant plant with purple branches and flowers, and a slight cinnamon scent. Dried, it makes a refreshing digestive tea. It can also be used in desserts (custard, sherbet). Plant tight for best effect, in rich well-drained soil.

Thai "Siam Queen" basil: gorgeous as a border, this compact (1 ft/30 cm) basil produces large clusters of pink and mauve flowers among the dark green foliage. Leaves have a nice licorice taste that goes well with oriental cooking. I steep flower heads in apple cider vinegar, which turns to a lovely pink color.

Wonderful in vinaigrettes.

"African blue" basil: similar to cinnamon basil in appearance, it is quite decorative but I do not care for the taste.

Lemon basil: compact, with small leaves, this basil bursts with lemon fragrance and is a flavorful addition to salads, herbal teas and lemonades. Perfect for grilling fish too! I always had trouble growing plants from seeds until I tried "Sweet Dani". This lemon basil grows without fuss into a small bush, 2 ft (60 cm) high, and produces almost twice as much essential oil as standard lemon basil. Plants can be trimmed for harvest several times with excellent regrowth. Most importantly, the strong lemon flavor is preserved when the basil is dried.

Pistou and pesto

One is with pine nuts — pesto — and the other without. Both have basil as the main ingredient and both names come from the Italian *pestare*, meaning to crush.

Traditionally, the crushing is done with a mortar and pestle. It is the best way to bring out the basil's flavor and I recommend it when making small batches. But a food processor allows you to make large batches in no time at all.

Fill the bowl of a food processor with fresh clean basil leaves. Process by pulses to chop coarsely, add 3-4 garlic cloves (minced or crushed with a garlic press), salt and pepper to taste. Process at low speed while adding olive oil in a slow stream until you get a soft paste. Add grated Parmesan (about 1 cup/250 ml), pine nuts (1/2 cup/125 ml), more oil and process to a paste.

Use to flavor pasta dishes and soups, or spread on a half baguette and broil a few seconds.

When making pesto for freezing, omit garlic (it becomes bitter) and Parmesan (it gets clumpy). Add them before serving.

Basil-tomato paste

To the traditional pesto, I prefer tomato paste for freezing, as the acidity of the tomatoes preserves the full flavor of basil as well as its bright green color.

Choose fleshy tomatoes that are ripe but still firm. Italian or plum tomatoes are best. Cut in half or in wedges if large. Place on a baking sheet, skin-side down. Bake at 200 °F (95 °C) for 4 hours. The tomatoes should be leathery, not dry.

Fill the bowl of a food processor loosely with basil leaves. Process by pulses until coarsely chopped. Add enough baked tomatoes to fill the bowl halfway. Purée at high speed, then add about 1 cup (250 ml) of olive oil in a steady stream while processing at medium speed. Season to taste.

For freezing, line ramekin molds or teacups with plastic film, leaving about 1 inch (3 cm) hanging out. Fill with tomato paste, fold film over and freeze. Unmold and keep in a freezer bag.

I use this tomato paste — it is not yet pesto — for my two favorite snacks.

Avocado-basil sandwich

INGREDIENTS

1/2 baguette

1/2 cup (125 ml) tomato-basil paste

4 lettuce leaves

1 ripe avocado

Salt, pepper

Olive oil

Lemon juice

Slice bread in half lengthwise. Spread tomato-basil paste on the bottom portion. Cover with lettuce leaves.

Peel avocado, remove stone and slice. Arrange slices over lettuce, drizzle with olive oil and lemon juice, season to taste.

You may add sliced radishes and fresh basil leaves.

Minute pizza

INGREDIENTS

1 large pita or chapatti bread

1 cup (250 ml) tomato-basil paste

1 cup (250 ml) grated mozzarella

Olive oil

Spread paste on pita, sprinkle with cheese and drizzle with olive oil. Broil until cheese is melted.

You can add ham or pepperoni, mushrooms, black olives or anchovies.

Avocado-basil sandwich

Spring greens and berry salad

I grow two kinds of lettuce, mizuna, a slender leafed and mild flavored oriental green, and arugula, also known as roquette, with a strong peppery taste and pretty flowers. But I use many other greens as well throughout the growing season.

This salad, for example, is composed of young tender kale, beet and radish greens. Pears add sweetness to the tangy leaves and strawberries give the salad a spring flavor.

I serve the vinaigrette separately.

A variation of this salad could include nasturtium leaves, broccoli and chive flowers, arugula, chervil, basil, apples and red currants.

VINAIGRETTE

Combined with ricotta or sour cream, this vinaigrette makes a quick dip for raw veggies.

INGREDIENTS

1 tbsp. (15 ml) French mustard

2 tbsp. (30 ml) lemon juice

1/2 tsp. (2.5 ml) salt

1/2 cup (125 ml) olive oil

2 tbsp. (30 ml) fresh herbs: basil, tarragon, and chives, minced

Combine mustard, lemon juice and salt. Beat in oil.

Taste and add salt if necessary, or lemon juice if the emulsion is too thick.

Add fresh herbs last. Serve on the side or drizzle on the salad just before serving, as some leaves wilt rapidly and fruit soften when in contact with an acid dressing.

Mexican salad

*I always keep a few cans of beans —
white or black beans, chickpeas,
flageolets, fava beans — in my pantry
to prepare quick nutritious salads,
soups or vegetarian dishes.*

INGREDIENTS

Olive oil

2 red bell peppers

1 summer squash: crookneck,
zucchini, petty pan

2 cans black beans (15 oz/425 g
each)

1 green onion, minced

1/2 cup (125 ml) fresh coriander
leaves, minced

Grated peel and juice of 1 lime

Dice squash and bell peppers.

Heat 2-3 tbsp. olive oil in a skillet
and stir-fry peppers until the skin
starts to sizzle and darken. Remove
with a slotted spoon and reserve.

Add more oil if necessary and stir-fry
squash until crisp on all sides. Turn
off the heat, cover the skillet and let
stand 5 minutes, enough time to cook
the squash thoroughly without
making it mushy.

Meanwhile, drain and rinse black
beans.

Combine all ingredients in a large
serving bowl, season to taste and mix
well. Let stand in a cool place for
1-2 hours before serving.

SERVES 4-6.

Coriander

Coriander is definitely not
everybody's herb. Some people love
it — I am among them — while
others strongly dislike its pungent
aroma, reminiscent of bug juice. Not
surprisingly, its name derives from
the Greek word *koros*, meaning
a bug.

Also known as cilantro and Chinese
parsley, coriander has a convoluted
past. Native to the Middle East, it is
mentioned in the Bible as one of the
sacred bitter herbs. Romans used it
to preserve meat and it was grown in

Charlemagne's garden.

Yet ancient physicians were quite
ambivalent about coriander. Some
considered it poisonous, others
believed it could cure the plague
and epilepsy, and make childbirth
painless. Some called it aphrodisiac
and others soothing. Quite confusing
indeed!

Today, coriander is used in Latin
American, eastern and oriental
cuisines. Peruvians are so fond of
this herb that it is used in almost
all their dishes.

Both leaves and dried seeds are used, but not interchangeably, as they taste quite different from one another. Fresh coriander leaves (and green seeds) have a strikingly fetid smell with a hint of licorice. They add flavor to Mexican and Tex-Mex dishes (salsa, guacamole, chili), oriental soups, rice and bean dishes. Add chopped leaves at the last minute to preserve their full aroma.

Dried seeds lose the fetid smell to develop a mild aromatic taste with a hint of orange peel. They are used in such liqueurs as Izarra and Chartreuse. Whole or crushed, they season venison marinades, curries, meat and vegetable stews. Finely ground, they add flavor to cakes and cookies. Chewing a few coriander seeds works wonders for garlic breath.

Gardening

Coriander is an annual of the *Umbelliferae* family, with erect stems, about 2 ft/60 cm high, and slender, with branches. The tiny white or mauve flowers are delicate and are a nice addition to flower beds as well as to vegetable gardens. It has a reputation for repelling aphids and helping anis germinate.

Coriander likes a sunny location and a light, sandy soil. It reseeds itself easily. Pick leaves when the plant is young. Use the flowers and green seeds as you do the leaves. Green seeds freeze well. Harvest dry seeds when brown, keep in airtight glass jars.

Papaya and nasturtium salad

Papaya is one of my favorite fruit. I find it especially refreshing in salad. Inside the fruit are little black seeds that look like very expensive caviar. They are also edible. Cleaned and dried, they can be used like peppercorns.

The first time I tasted the seeds, I immediately thought of nasturtiums. It was the same peppery, piquant flavor. The uncanny resemblance between the two inspired this colorful salad, which never fails to surprise and delight my guests.

Peel and cut one large (or two medium) papaya in half lengthwise. Remove seeds and cut in large cubes.

Prepare the vinaigrette (page 59) replacing lemon juice with lime juice and using herbs such as lemon basil, Thai basil, lemon balm and a dash of ginger if you wish.

Toss papaya with vinaigrette and let stand 1 hour.

Pick about 2 cups (500 ml) of nasturtium leaves and cut into ribbons. Arrange on serving plate, place papaya on top, garnish with nasturtium leaves* and serve.

SERVES 2-4.

* *Nasturtium leaves and flowers have purgative, tonic and antiseptic properties. They also contain antibiotic substances. People who have trouble eating watercress should also avoid nasturtiums.*

Flower tabouleh

Flowers change with the seasons. In spring, my tabouleh includes violet, pansy, chive, dandelion and tulip petals. This one is a summer tabouleh.

INGREDIENTS

2 cups (500 ml) water

1 tsp. (5 ml) salt

2 cups (500 ml) couscous semolina (medium)

1/2 cup (125 ml) fresh coriander and/or parsley, chopped

1/4 cup (65 ml) mint leaves, chopped

2 cups (500 ml) petals: nasturtium, cornflower, calendula, miniature marigold, evening primrose, coriander, basil and arugula flowers

1/2 cup (125 ml) olive oil

Juice of 1 lemon or 2 limes

Salt, pepper

Bring water and salt to a boil. Add couscous all at once, cover and remove from heat. Let stand about 10 minutes, until all water has been absorbed. Loosen couscous with a fork and cool.

You can also cook couscous in the microwave oven. Combine water, salt and couscous. Cook 2-3 minutes at maximum until all water has been absorbed. Cool.

Combine couscous with herbs and flowers. Drizzle with olive oil and lemon juice, season to taste and mix gently. Serve.

SERVES 3-4.

Thai salad

An oriental mandolin (vegetable slicer) allows you to cut the cucumber and radish in long thin strips akin to spaghetti. I love that gadget! But if oriental grocery stores are scarce in your neighborhood, just grate the radish with a cheese grater and cut the cucumber by hand.

INGREDIENTS

1 seedless cucumber

1 small daikon (white Chinese radish) or a bouquet of pink radishes

1/2 lb (250 g) rice noodles

4 tbsp. (60 ml) sesame oil

ORIENTAL VINAIGRETTE:

4 tbsp. (60 ml) soy sauce

2 tbsp. (30 ml) balsamic vinegar

1 tsp. (5 ml) French mustard

1/2 cup (125 ml) fresh coriander or Thai basil, chopped

Juice and peel of 1 lime

Pepper

Peel cucumber and radish, cut into long thin strips.

Bring 4 cups (1 liter) of water with 1 tsp. (5 ml) salt to a boil. Throw in noodles, remove from heat and let stand 10 to 15 minutes until tender. Rinse under cold water, drain well and toss with sesame oil to prevent noodles from sticking.

Combine all vinaigrette ingredients and mix well.

Arrange noodles in individual bowls, top with cucumber and radish, and drizzle with vinaigrette. Garnish with marigold or calendula petals.

Feta and broccoli salad

Here's a way to prepare a light yet nutritious meal in just minutes. Combine feta — or another type of cheese — with seasonal vegetables and herbs. Here are some ideas.

Greek salad: tomatoes, feta, cucumber, onion, black olives and basil.

French open: warm potatoes, feta, hard-boiled egg, quartered, and tarragon.

Polish classic: cooked beets cut in cubes, chickpeas (or black beans), feta and lots of chive flowers.

FOR THIS RECIPE:

2 cups (500 ml) broccoli florets

1 cup (250 ml) feta, cubed or crumbled

12 black olives

1 cup (250 ml) vinaigrette (page 59)

Arugula flowers for garnish

Steam broccoli 5 minutes or microwave 2 minutes, until cooked but still firm. Rinse under cold running water to preserve color, then drain.

Combine all ingredients and let stand 30 minutes before serving.

SERVES 2.

Flageolet and herb chicken salad

Flageolet and herb chicken salad

INGREDIENTS

2 parsnips

1 small fennel bulb

Olive oil

1/4 cup (65 ml) white vermouth (Noilly Prat*) or white wine

2 cups (500 ml) canned flageolets or white beans, drained and rinsed

1/2 lb (250 g) chicken breast, deboned and skin removed

1 tbsp. (15 ml) mixed dried herbs (see page 12)

Salt, pepper

Peel parsnips and cut into sticks. Cut fennel in half, remove tough bottom part, then cut in thick slices.

Heat 2 tbsp. (30 ml) oil in a skillet, stir-fry parsnips 2-3 minutes. Add fennel and stir-fry until sizzling. Add vermouth, cover and cook 1 minute.

Add flageolets, season to taste and heat through. Arrange on serving plates and set aside.

Clean skillet and heat 2 tbsp. (30 ml) oil. Brown chicken breast 2-3 minutes on each side over high heat. Season with herbs, salt and pepper. Cover and cook 2-4 minutes, until chicken is done.

Remove from pan and let stand a few minutes before slicing chicken into strips. Arrange over vegetables and serve warm or cold.

SERVES 4.

* Noilly Prat vermouth

I make great use of white vermouth, not for dry martinis but to deglaze pans, as a reduction for sauces, and to replace sherry or rice wine in oriental dishes. I find it more practical to keep a bottle of vermouth in the pantry than to open a bottle of white wine every time I need one cup for cooking. Though, like wine, vermouth declines in quality once the bottle is open, it remains perfectly usable for culinary purposes.

There are other white vermouths, mainly Italian, but my favorite is French Noilly Prat. Produced in Marseillan, this fine aromatized wine is drier than Italian vermouth, with an exceptional aroma due to its unique method of production. It is made from Picpoul and Clairette, the fruity wines of southern France, which first go through various stages of maturation in oak barrels, including one year in the open air. Improved by sun, sea breeze and variations in temperature, the wines are then blended and combined with herbs, spices and fruit spirits. This is what makes Noilly Prat so useful in the kitchen.

Trout with cream sauce and tulips

Botanical tulips have a slight peppery flavor and are great in salads. But their colors are often quite intense. For this delicate dish, I have chosen a hybrid tulip — rather tasteless, I admit, but just the right color.

INGREDIENTS

8 tulips, preferably pink

2 tbsp. (30 ml) butter

4 trout fillets

1/4 cup (65 ml) heavy cream

Salt, pepper

Pluck petals from stem and cut the bitter white base. Cut in ribbons.

In a skillet, melt butter and cook fish over medium heat, 3 minutes on each side or until done. Remove from skillet and keep warm.

Add cream to skillet and bring rapidly to a boil. Season with salt and pepper.

Place trout fillets on warm plates, spoon sauce over and decorate with tulips.

SERVES 4.

Breaded veal with daisy bud and tomato sauce

I use wild ox-eye daisy — not the garden variety — that I pick in fields around my house.

An excellent addition to salads, the spring leaves and shoots are crunchy with a light licorice flavor. In early summer, I pick young buds to flavor vinegars and sauces. I also dry just-opened flowers for herbal teas.

INGREDIENTS

1 onion, minced

3 cups (750 ml) tomatoes, peeled, seeded and coarsely chopped

12 black olives, pitted (optional)

1 cup (250 ml) daisy buds

4 veal escalopes, flattened

1 egg, beaten

1 cup (250 ml) dry breadcrumbs

Salt, pepper

Olive oil

In a heavy saucepan, heat 2 tbsp. (30 ml) oil and cook onion until soft, about 1 minute.

Add tomatoes, olives and daisy buds. Season with salt and pepper and cook over high heat, 5 minutes or until thickened. Cover and reserve.

Dip veal in beaten egg and coat with breadcrumbs. In a skillet, heat some oil and cook escalopes over medium heat, 2-3 minutes each side or until done.

Arrange on warmed serving plates and spoon sauce over.

SERVES 4.

Variation:
* *If daisy buds are unavailable, use 1/4 cup (65 ml) chopped capers.*
* *Serve the sauce over grilled fish or chicken.*

Lamb chops with beebalm

INGREDIENTS

2 tbsp. (30 ml) cooking oil

4 lamb chops

1/2 cup (125 ml) white vermouth, preferably Noilly Prat

1/2 cup (125 ml) beebalm petals

Salt, pepper

Preheat the oven to 300 °F (150 °C).

In a skillet, heat the oil and brown chops 2-3 minutes each side. Reserve in warm oven.

Deglaze skillet with vermouth, scraping the bottom to loosen sediments. Cook 1 minute over high heat, season to taste and add beebalm petals.

Pour sauce over lamb chops and serve with green beans.

SERVES 4.

Beebalm

In 1773, when American settlers got fed up with unjust taxes and threw all the tea in Boston's harbor, they started the movement for Independence — and an acute shortage of their favorite drink. Fortunately, Oswego Indians knew of a plant with aromatic leaves that could be a satisfactory substitute. Soon, Boston high society was converted to Oswego tea. The plant was beebalm or *Monarda didyma*.

Sometimes called bergamot, though it has no relation with the citrus fruit of the same name, beebalm is native to eastern North America and owes its name to Nicolas Monardes, a 16th century Spanish doctor who was the first to identify the plant. Besides the Indians, of course!

The garden variety is a tall, exuberant perennial with red, pink or purple flowers. A new hybrid with white flowers is sometimes available in nurseries. Easy to grow in sun or partial shade and a moist soil, it is often afflicted with mildew and should be planted at the back of a flowerbed. Leaves and flowers are very aromatic, with a spicy, minty fragrance. Beebalm has digestive properties and the *Monarda punctata* species was used extensively in Indian medicine.

Beebalm makes an excellent herbal tea but can also be used in a multitude of sweet and savory dishes. Use chopped leaves sparingly — the flavor is quite powerful — in stuffings and salads. Sprinkle petals over fruit salads or add to cakes, pancake batter, cookies and custard. To freeze petals, spread on a cookie sheet and freeze. Store in a rigid container.

Chicken breast with raspberry-mango sauce

Raspberries and mangoes are in season at the same time — early summer — and they go so well together I was inspired to create this recipe.

INGREDIENTS

2 tbsp. (30 ml) sugar

1/4 cup (65 ml) raspberry vinegar

1/4 cup (65 ml) raspberry liqueur

1 cup (250 ml) fresh raspberries

1 tbsp. (30 ml) butter

1 tbsp. (30 ml) oil

2 chicken breasts, halved

1 ripe mango, peeled and sliced

Salt, pepper

In a small heavy saucepan, combine sugar, vinegar and liqueur. Bring to a boil and add half of the fresh raspberries. Reduce heat and simmer 10 minutes, while stirring and crushing the fruit. Strain through a fine sieve and reserve.

In a large non-adhesive frying pan, heat butter and oil. Fry chicken 1 minute on each side. Season to taste.

Add mango slices and raspberry sauce, cover and simmer 5 to 8 minutes — depending on the thickness of the meat — until done.

Add remaining raspberries, reheat a few seconds and serve with calendula risotto (page 45) or tarragon noodles (page 49).

SERVES 4.

Raspberry vinegar

Fill a glass jar halfway with fresh raspberries, top with natural cider vinegar. Seal and keep in a cool, dry place for 1 month, stirring the jar from time to time. Strain and keep in a sealed bottle.

Raspberry liqueur

Proceed as above, replacing vinegar with vodka. Strain through cheesecloth and add a sugar-water syrup. The amount of sugar depends on your "sweet tooth", the amount of water on the degree of alcohol you wish your liqueur to have. Drink within 3 months.

Veal kidneys with gooseberries

INGREDIENTS

1.5 lb (700 g) veal kidneys

2 tbsp. (30 ml) butter

1/4 cup (65 ml) brandy

1 cup (250 ml) ripe gooseberries

1/4 cup (65 ml) heavy cream

Salt, pepper

Cut kidneys into bite-sized pieces, removing the tough white membranes. Rinse under cold running water and pat dry.

In a large skillet, heat butter, add kidneys and cook, stirring over medium heat for 30 seconds. Flame with brandy, cover and simmer 2-3 minutes. The meat should stay pink inside.

Remove kidneys with a slotted spoon and keep warm.

Add gooseberries to the skillet, bring to a boil and cook over high heat until reduced by half. Add cream, season to taste, and cook, stirring constantly until sauce has thickened. Transfer meat to the sauce and reheat gently.

Serve with rice or creamy mashed potatoes.

SERVES 4.

Lamb with lemon verbena

Mangoes and papayas contain meat-tenderizing enzymes. Employing them in cooking allows you to use tougher but tastier meat cuts.

INGREDIENTS

1 large mango (or 1 small + 1 small papaya)

1 cup (250 ml) white vermouth, preferably Noilly Prat

1/4 cup (65 ml) cooking oil

2 medium onions, minced

2 lb (1 kg) lamb, neck or shoulder, cubed

1 small chili pepper, seeded and minced*

1 cup (250 ml) fresh lemon verbena leaves

Salt, pepper

* Use gloves to seed and mince chili pepper.

Peel and remove stone from mango. In a blender, purée mango flesh with vermouth. Reserve.

In a heavy-based pan or flameproof casserole, heat the oil and cook onions until soft, about 2 minutes. Add meat and brown on all sides. Add puréed mango, chili pepper and lemon verbena leaves sealed in cheesecloth, salt and pepper to taste.

Cover and simmer over very low heat for 1 hour or until meat is tender. Remove bag of leaves and adjust seasoning.

If the sauce is too thin, thicken with *beurre manié* (a paste made of equal parts butter and flour).

If using a pressure cooker, reduce vermouth by half and cook 15 minutes.

Serve over a bed of rice.

SERVES 4-6.

Lemon verbena

We know lemon verbena — often associated with mint — as a herbal tea. But lemon verbena is also, and above all, a beautiful shrub reaching 15 feet (4 1/2 m) high in its native Chile. In cold climates, it should be grown in a pot and brought indoors in winter.

My lemon verbena, shown here at the tender age of three, is now a much larger five year old, with a 3 feet (1 m) span. I trim the branches two or three times during the growing season. Tender leaves are frozen for culinary use, tougher ones are dried for tea.

In the kitchen, I use lemon verbena in much the same way I use scented geranium, to add fragrance to steamed chicken or fish (see Barbecued Shark, page 82) and to flavor desserts such as rice pudding, custard and *crème brûlée.*

Lemon verbena is soothing and helps digestion, a good reason to use it in cooking.

Rabbit with tarragon sauce

A French country cooking classic,
this recipe is also suitable for chicken.

INGREDIENTS

1/3 cup (85 ml) cooking oil

1 onion, minced

2 tbsp. (15 ml) flour

1 rabbit (2 to 3 lb/1 to 1.5 kg)
in pieces

1 tsp. (5 ml) salt

1/2 cup (125 ml) fresh tarragon
leaves

2 cups white wine

Pepper

In a heavy pot or flameproof casserole, heat oil and cook onion until soft, about 2 minutes. Coat meat with flour and shake off excess. Fry quickly until browned on all sides. Add tarragon and wine. Season with salt and pepper. Cover and simmer over very low heat for 1 hour or until meat is tender.

You may want to remove the saddle pieces after 40 minutes, as they cook faster than the thighs.

With a pressure cooker, use only 1 cup of wine and cook 15 minutes.

SERVES 4-6.

Tarragon

Tarragon is a "must" in the kitchen. Its cool, refreshing taste is well-suited to egg, chicken and fish dishes. It adds zing to any salad, and flavor to vinegars and sauces as well as desserts.

Its elegant foliage gives it the right to grow in one of my flowerbeds alongside black-eyed Susans. A hardy perennial, tarragon loves dry, sunny places. There are two kinds of tarragon: Russian tarragon, a native of Siberia, which is rather tasteless, and French tarragon from southern Europe, much more aromatic and the one to use in cooking.

Pick young, tender leaves throughout the growing season. Freeze but do not dry, as the flavor is lost during the process.

BBQ fish

Whether fresh or dried, aromatic herbs are a "must" when grilling on the barbecue.

Here, a sea bream has been coated with olive oil and a blend of sesame seeds, rock salt and crushed dried coriander seeds. Making incisions on both sides shortens the cooking time.

The shrimp were marinated about 30 minutes in lime juice, olive oil and fresh chopped coriander leaves, then grilled, 5 minutes per side.

Fresh herbs are well suited for steaming fish "en papillote"* — wrapped in foil packets. Fish cooked this way will steam gently and stay moist, while capturing the essence of the herbs.

For white fish I choose lemon or anise-scented herbs such as lemon balm, lemon basil, Thai basil, dill, anise hyssop. For salmon and trout I use lovage and tarragon.

Shark tastes very much like chicken, so I often use basil for this delicious but little known fish. Fillets of baby shark are best, as big specimens tend to be tough.

*"Papillote": Make a bed of fresh herbs — lemon basil and dill for example — place fish on top, drizzle with olive oil, season with salt and pepper, and cover with thin slices of lemon or lime. Wrap loosely.

Cook 10 to 15 minutes over medium heat, until fish flakes easily with a fork.

Serve with Romesco sauce (page 84) or Coriander salsa.

Coriander salsa

INGREDIENTS

1 ripe mango

1 ripe papaya

1 red bell pepper

1 green onion, minced

1/2 cup (125 ml) fresh coriander leaves, finely chopped

Grated peel and juice of 1 lime

Peel and remove stone and seeds from the fruit. Chop coarsely. Seed pepper and remove the bitter white membranes. Chop coarsely.

Combine all ingredients and let stand for at least 2 hours before serving.

MAKES ABOUT 2 CUPS (500 ML).

Steamed chicken with scented geranium

Steaming is a healthy but rather bland cooking method. By adding scented leaves — geranium, lemon verbena — the chicken (or fish) is infused with a delicate fragrance.

Steaming: Make a bed of scented leaves in a metal or bamboo steamer, place chicken fillet or breast on top, season with salt and pepper, and steam until done.

Microwave: make a bed of leaves in a shallow dish, place chicken on top, season, cover with more leaves, and add 2 tbsp. (30 ml) water or white wine. Cover with plastic film and microwave at maximum for 5-7 minutes, depending on the thickness of the meat.

Serve with Romesco sauce.

Romesco sauce

I first tasted this sauce in Spain where it is served with grilled baby leeks, called calçots. *Thumb-sized leeks are tied in large bundles and placed over an open fire. The outside layers get scorched while the ones inside become tender. One eats the leek by holding it between thumb and forefinger, using the other hand to delicately pull out the center and dunk it in Romesco sauce. Fabulous!*

INGREDIENTS

4 red bell peppers
1 small fresh chili pepper
2 garlic heads
1/2 cup (125 ml) olive oil
Salt, pepper

Place peppers in a pie plate or shallow baking dish and bake at 375 °F (190 °C), turning them over regularly until the skin blisters and blackens, about 1 hour. Cool slightly, remove skin and seeds.

Peel garlic and place in a small ovenproof dish, cover with olive oil and wrap with aluminum foil. Cook at the same time as the bell peppers. Garlic should be soft when peppers are cooked.

Combine peppers and garlic in a

blender and process until creamy. Season with salt and pepper to taste. Add a little olive oil if the sauce is too thick, or reserve to season salads.

MAKES ABOUT 2 CUPS (500 ML).

Note: Romesco sauce freezes well.

Scented geranium

Scented geranium is not a real geranium but a member of the *pelargonium* family. It comes in various flavors, lime, chocolate, coconut, all of them edible. But I only use the lemon-scented kind for culinary purposes.

I grow a few plants in the garden and one in a pot to bring indoors in the fall as it is a tender perennial and would not survive our harsh winters. Placed in a cool, sunny location, the plant provides me with cuttings for new plants in spring.

I harvest leaves throughout the growing season, to use fresh or to freeze (raw in freezer bags).

Stuffed chicken en crapaudine

"En crapaudine" means "like a toad" — and a chicken when split and flattened does look like a toad. This cooking method allows the meat to keep its flavor and prevents it from drying.

INGREDIENTS

1 roasting chicken, about 3 lb (1.5 kg)
2 oz (100 g) feta cheese
3 tbsp. (45 ml) fresh herbs, chopped or 1 tbsp. dried herbs (your choice)
Olive oil
1 onion, minced
10 garlic cloves
Salt, pepper

Preheat the oven to 375 °F (190 °C).

With kitchen scissors or a sharp knife, split the bird open down one side of the backbone. Cut the other side and remove the backbone. Turn over and flatten with the palm of your hand.

Pinch the skin, then insert your hand between skin and flesh to loosen.

Mash feta cheese with a fork and mix with herbs and 1 tbsp. (15 ml) olive oil. Spread paste under the skin.

In a shallow, ovenproof dish, make a bed of onion and garlic, place chicken on top, drizzle with olive oil, season with salt and pepper and add a few tbsp. water or white wine to the pan. Cover and bake for 45 minutes. Uncover and cook another 30 minutes or until chicken is done.

SERVES 4.

Chicken and lovage pot-au-feu

Here is a complete meal ready in less than 30 minutes using a pressure cooker.

STUFFING:

2 cups (500 ml) raw spinach or kale, chopped

1/2 cup (125 ml) uncooked rice

1 egg

1 tbsp. (15 ml) salt

2 tbsp. (30 ml) herbs, chopped

1 chicken, 3 lb (1.5 kg)

2 cups (500 ml) water

4 baby turnips

4 carrots

2 potatoes

2 lovage stalks

1 bay leaf

Salt, pepper

Combine stuffing ingredients and fill chicken loosely as the rice will swell during cooking. Truss securely with kitchen string or bamboo skewers.

Place chicken and remaining ingredients in a pressure cooker, season to taste and cook 15 minutes. Or place chicken, water and seasoning in a large stock pot and simmer 1 hour. Add vegetables and cook another 30 minutes.

To check if the meat is done, prick the chicken between thigh and breast with a sharp knife or skewer. The juices should run clear.

Serve the broth with croutons and grated Parmesan cheese as a first course, then the chicken and vegetables with Gribiche or Romesco sauce (page 84).

SERVES 4.

Gribiche sauce

INGREDIENTS

1 hard-boiled egg

1 tbsp. (15 ml) tarragon vinegar or lemon juice

1 tbsp. (15 ml) French mustard

1 cup (250 ml) olive oil

1 tbsp. (15 ml) of each — parsley, chervil, tarragon, basil, lovage — chopped

1 tbsp. (15 ml) capers, chopped

Mash the egg yolk with a fork and combine with vinegar and mustard. Add oil gradually, beating constantly as for a mayonnaise. Add herbs, capers and chopped egg white.

Gribiche sauce is often served with boiled tongue.

Lovage

Lovage is a hardy, ornamental perennial and one of the best culinary herbs. Yet it is seldom grown in gardens. Is this because it grows to huge proportions and, like rhubarb, is almost impossible to budge once it puts down roots? Or is it simply because lovage has yet to be discovered by modern chefs?

Greek and Roman cooks used it extensively and 14th century doctors praised its diuretic and stimulant action. An old-fashioned cordial was brewed from lovage, yarrow and tansy.

It is the first herb to show green shoots in the spring and the last to disappear in late fall. Young tender leaves can be picked throughout the growing season, to use raw or cooked. When dried, lovage retains its strong celery-like flavor and it freezes well too.

A handful of leaves transforms a plain vegetable soup into a grand minestrone. Raw and chopped, they can be added — though sparingly, because of the strong taste — to salads, sauces, stews and stuffings. Lovage goes well with fish, especially salmon.

After a few years, the plant blooms,
sending a long spike over the bright
green foliage. Harvest seeds when
green for freezing and brown for
drying.

Crush dried seeds and combine with
sea salt as a substitute for celery salt.

Use frozen seeds and leaves to
flavor broth, vegetables, fish stock
and sauces.

Roasted leg of lamb with feta and pesto

INGREDIENTS

1 leg of lamb, about 5 lb (2.5 kg)

8 garlic cloves

2 oz (100 g) creamy feta or goat cheese

1/2 cup (125 ml) tomato-basil paste (page 54)

1 onion, minced

Olive oil

Salt, pepper

Fresh or dried chopped herbs: rosemary, thyme, oregano

Ask your butcher to remove the femur.

Preheat the oven to 400 °F (200 °C).

Peel garlic cloves. Pierce meat with a sharp knife and insert garlic cloves.

Mix together cheese and tomato paste. Spoon into the hole left by the bone, reserving about 2 tbsp (30 ml). Close hole with kitchen string or bamboo skewers.

Make a bed of onion in an ovenproof dish, add 1/4 cup (65 ml) water and set leg on top. Smear lamb with remaining cheese and tomato paste, drizzle with olive oil, season with salt and pepper, sprinkle generously with herbs.

Bake 15 minutes. Lower oven temperature to 350 °F (180 °C) and cook another 45 minutes to 1 hour — meat should stay pink — adding more water to the pan if necessary to prevent scorching. When lamb is cooked, let stand 5 minutes before carving.

Serve with roasted garlic.

SERVES 8.

Roasted garlic

When baked, garlic becomes sweet and more digestible, while losing its overpowering smell.

INGREDIENTS

4 garlic heads (or more)

Olive oil

Salt, pepper

Preheat the oven to 375 °F (190 °C).

Cut the top of the garlic heads but do not peel. Place on a bed of rosemary sprigs, in a shallow baking dish or a garlic baker*. Drizzle generously with olive oil, season with salt and pepper. Wrap dish with aluminum foil or cover with lid and bake 30-40 minutes with the lamb, until garlic is soft and golden.

To eat, remove the cloves with a spoon or fork and spread on toast.

* Garlic bakers are special earthenware dishes, pretty enough to bring to the table.

Lamb shanks with onion and apple compote

INGREDIENTS

Olive oil

4 lamb shanks, 12 to 14 oz (350 to 400 g) each

4 large onions, minced

1 cup (250 ml) apple juice

4 rosemary sprigs

1 apple, peeled and sliced

Salt, pepper

Preheat the oven to 350 °F (180 °C).

In a skillet, heat some oil and brown meat on all sides. Transfer to a large ovenproof dish.

Add more oil to the skillet if necessary and cook onions over medium heat, until soft. Transfer to baking dish.

Insert rosemary sprigs among shanks, add apple juice, season with salt and pepper. Cover and bake for 1 1/2 hours or until meat is done.

Ladle cooking juice into a small saucepan while keeping meat warm. Reduce cooking juice by a third over high heat. Add sliced apple and poach 5-10 minutes over medium heat. Adjust seasoning.

Arrange lamb shanks and apple compote on warmed serving plates, coat with gravy. Serve with grilled polenta, barley or brown rice.

SERVES 4.

Rosemary

Its Latin name means "sea dew", maybe because rosemary is native to the Mediterranean and loves salty breeze, or because its tiny luminous flowers evoke the color of the sea.

Renowned since the time of antiquity, rosemary was once purported to strengthen the memory and became a symbol of fidelity for lovers. Elizabeth, Queen of Hungary, is said to have kept her youth and beauty with the help of an elixir she prepared herself, using lavender, rosemary and mint. Dated 1235 in the Queen's handwriting, the formula is preserved in Vienna. "Hungary water", as it was known, became hugely popular in the 18th century and Madame de Sévigné is said to have employed liberal amounts.

Rosemary is a stimulant for the nervous system. It boosts morale and truly does strengthen memory. As a tonic, it facilitates digestion and liver functions. It is also an antiseptic.

In the kitchen, rosemary is an excellent accompaniment for grilled

or roasted meat, especially lamb. It adds flavor to stews, venison marinades, oils, vinegars and jellies. Use sparingly, especially in conjunction with other herbs, for it is powerful.

Fresh rosemary keeps well in a sealed plastic bag in the fridge. It retains all its flavor when dried.

Rosemary grows wild in Provence and along the Mediterranean coast. It loves warmth, sun and chalky soil. A tender perennial, it is best grown in a pot in colder regions and, brought indoors during winter, it will bloom in abundance. Choose a large container to avoid transplanting, which is always traumatic for

rosemary. With TLC and lots of sunshine, your rosemary bush will last many years. With careful trimming, you can shape it like a topiary or a bonsai. The twisted trunk and rough bark are especially suited to this oriental art form.

Sage

"Why should a man die whilst sage grows in his garden?" This wise saying is attributed to Tortula, a female doctor and member of the reputed School of Salerno.

The name derives from the Latin *salvus*, meaning "saved" or "safe", alluding to its solid reputation as a remedy. Before finding its rightful place in the kitchen, sage had been used to treat fevers, liver complaints, kidney troubles, colds, measles, rheumatic pains, headaches, throat problems and many other ailments.

Sacred to the Romans and a magic herb for the Celts, sage was prized by the Arabs and the Chinese, who would gladly exchange two crates of tea for one of sage. In the Middle Ages, people believed it could cure disease, protect from evil and even raise the dead.

THE GOURMET'S GARDEN   95

Saltimbocca

INGREDIENTS

4 veal escalopes

4 slices prosciutto

8 sage leaves

1 tbsp. (15 ml) olive oil

1 cup (250 ml) button mushrooms, quartered

1/4 cup (65 ml) white wine or white vermouth (Noilly Prat)

1/4 cup (65 ml) heavy cream

Salt, pepper

Flatten escalopes. Place a slice of prosciutto and 2 sage leaves on top of each, roll and secure with a toothpick.

In a skillet, heat the oil and brown rolls on all sides, about 1 minute. Add mushrooms and white wine. Season with salt and pepper, cover and simmer 8-10 minutes.

Remove rolls and mushrooms with a slotted spoon. Reduce cooking liquid over high heat until syrupy. Add cream, heat through and pour over saltimbocca.

Serve with orzo or risotto.

Serves 2.

Variation: Replace sage with fresh marjoram. Top prosciutto with cheese — provolone, fontina, gruyère — thinly sliced.

In the kitchen, sage is the choice herb for fatty meat — goose, duck, pork, mutton — as well as sausages and cold cuts. The British use it in stuffing and to flavor Derby cheese. Germans associate it with eel, Italians with veal.

Native to the Mediterranean basin, sage is a lovely plant with silvery leaves and tiny blue flowers. It grows best in full sun and light, sandy, well-drained soil. A tender perennial, it may not survive harsh winters. To increase its chances of survival, plant sage close to the house — along a south wall, for example — and cover with a thick mulch in the fall. Or grow in a container to bring indoors during winter, and keep it in a sunny, cool location.

There are several types of sage available from nurseries, with gold or purple leaves or a pineapple scent. These horticultural curiosities are grown more for their decorative foliage than for cooking. Pineapple sage produces tiny bright red flowers. It has limited use as a herbal tea.

Blackberries with beebalm

*I often prepare this spectacular dessert when I have unexpected guests.
While touring the garden with them, I pick the flowers and berries. Back in the
kitchen, I whip some cream and voilà!*

*Don't forget to cut off the green tip of the gladiolus and remove the stamens
and pistils before filling.*

Fruit salad with beebalm

Beebalm has a strong, spicy, minty taste that goes well with lamb chops (page 73) as well as with this fruit salad.

Here, I combined three types of melons and raspberries, but you may use other fruit. I crushed a handful of beebalm petals in a mortar with sugar and sprinkled the mixture over the fruit. Chilled one hour and garnished with whole petals, this fruit salad is elegant and refreshing.

Beebalm shortbreads

INGREDIENTS

2 cups (500 ml) all-purpose flour

2 tbsp. (30 ml) butter

1/2 tbsp. (7.5 ml) baking powder

Pinch of salt

1/2 cup (125 ml) beebalm petals, loosely packed

1 egg

1/3 cup (85 ml) buttermilk

1/3 cup (85 ml) melted butter

Preheat the oven to 400 °F (200 °C).

Combine flour, sugar, baking powder, salt and beebalm.

Beat together egg, buttermilk and melted butter. Combine with dry ingredients until you get a soft dough. Do not overwork.

Spread to a 1 inch (2 cm) thickness. Cut with cookie cutters and place on a cookie sheet.

Bake 15 minutes or until slightly golden. Transfer to a cooling rack.

Serve with strawberry-beebalm jam.

MAKES 12-18 SHORTBREADS.

Strawberry-beebalm jam

INGREDIENTS

4 cups (1 liter) strawberries, crushed

3 cups (750 ml) sugar

1/2 cup (125 ml) beebalm petals

Combine strawberries and sugar in a heavy pot and bring slowly to a boil. Cook over medium heat, stirring constantly, until thick (about 30 minutes). Add beebalm last.

Skim foam if necessary and ladle into hot, sterilized jars. Seal.

MAKES ABOUT 4 X 1 CUP (250 ML) JARS.

Valentine's day cake

Frozen geranium leaves are better than fresh leaves for this cake, as with other baked goods. When reduced to powder with a food processor or blender, frozen leaves have a fine icy texture that blends well with the dough and melts during cooking.

INGREDIENTS

2/3 cup (170 ml) sugar

1/3 cup (65 ml) soft butter

3 eggs, separated

1/4 cup (65 ml) frozen scented geranium leaves, reduced to powder

1 cup (250 ml) all-purpose flour

1 tbsp. (15 ml) baking powder

1 pinch salt

1/2 cup (125 ml) milk

FROSTING

3/4 cup (185 ml) heavy cream

2 tbsp. (30 ml) sugar

1 tbsp. (15 ml) kirsch (optional)

Cocoa powder

1/2 cup (125 ml) slivered almonds, roasted

Preheat the oven to 375 °F (190 °C).

Grease a heart-shaped mold.

Whisk together sugar and butter until creamy. Beat in egg yolks, then scented geranium.

Combine flour, baking powder and salt. Stir dry ingredients into egg mixture, alternating with milk.

Whip egg whites with salt until stiff and fold into mixture. Spoon into mold and bake 35 minutes or until a toothpick inserted in the middle comes out clean. Unmold and cool on a wire rack.

Whip cream to soft peaks, add sugar and liqueur, whip until stiff.

With a spatula, spread over top and sides of the cake. Dust with cocoa powder and sprinkle with roasted slivered almonds.

Serve with strawberry or raspberry coulis.

SERVES 6-8.

Coulis:
Crush 2-3 cups (500-750 ml) of berries or purée in a food processor. Strain raspberries only through a fine sieve, pressing the pulp with a spoon, to remove tiny seeds. Add sugar to taste.

Elderberry crepes

While elderberry florets and berries are edible, all green parts (stems, leaves and unripe fruit) are toxic.

INGREDIENTS

8 elderberry blossom clusters

1 cup (250 ml) milk

1 egg

1/2 cup (125 ml) all-purpose flour

Pinch of salt

1 tbsp. (15 ml) sugar

1 tsp. (5 ml) vanilla extract

1 tbsp. (15 ml) oil for batter + for cooking

Using a fork, detach florets from stems.

Combine all ingredients for the batter, except the florets, and let stand in a cool place for at least 1 hour.

Add florets and thin batter with milk if too thick. It should lightly coat the back of a spoon.

Using a paper wad dipped in oil, lightly grease a non-stick pan, pour in a small quantity of batter and twirl the pan to spread it into a thin layer. Cook about 1 minute until it starts to blister, and flip over. Repeat until all batter has been used. Sprinkle with sugar.

MAKES 8-10 CREPES.

Elderberry muffins

Elderberry florets can be dried and used to flavor muffins and cakes. Remove florets from stems, spread over a fine mesh (mosquito net is ideal) and place in a warm, dry place. When dried, store in a clean glass jar.

INGREDIENTS

2 eggs

1 cup (250 ml) oil

1 cup (250 ml) brown sugar

1 cup (250 ml) milk

1/2 tsp. (2.5 ml) vanilla extract

1 cup (250 ml) dried elderberry florets

2 cups (500 ml) all-purpose flour

1/2 tbsp. (7.5 ml) baking powder

1/2 tsp. (2.5 ml) salt

Preheat the oven to 375 °F (190 °C).

In a food processor or with an electric beater, beat eggs until pale in color, then add the oil in a slow steady stream, as for a mayonnaise.

Beat in sugar, milk, vanilla and florets.

Combine dry ingredients and stir into the batter. Beat until smooth.

Spoon into greased muffin tins and bake 25-30 minutes until golden.

MAKES 12 MUFFINS.

Lemon verbena custard

I love what the French call "crème anglaise", but the amount of egg yolks needed (6-8) always seemed excessive to me. So here is my own version, much healthier and foolproof.

INGREDIENTS

2 cups (500 ml) milk

1/4 cup (65 ml) fresh lemon verbena leaves

2 eggs

1/2 cup (125 ml) sugar

1 tbsp. (15 ml) corn starch

Simmer leaves in milk for 15 minutes. Strain and return to pan.

Beat together eggs, sugar and cornstarch. Stir in a little milk, then return the mixture to the pan with the remaining milk, and stir. Cook over low heat, stirring constantly with a wooden spoon until thick. Do not boil.

Variation: Replace verbena with scented geranium or flavor custard with orange blossom water.

MAKES ABOUT 2 CUPS.

Tip: To prevent the formation of a "skin" when the custard cools, cover with plastic film.

Berry tartlets

Doubling the quantity of cornstarch makes for a thick custard — crème anglaise becomes crème pâtissière — ideal for these scrumptious tartlets.

Spoon the thick custard into baked tartlet shells. Cool, then garnish with seasonal berries.

Berry tartlets

Berries au gratin

This elegant dessert is always a hit with guests. I prefer to use frozen berries as they remain partially frozen and make a startling contrast with the hot custard.

INGREDIENTS

2-3 cups (500-750 ml) fresh or frozen berries (strawberries, raspberries, blackberries, blueberries)

1 cup (250 ml) lemon verbena custard (page 104)

Sugar

Divide the berries among 4 ramekin molds, spoon custard over and sprinkle with sugar. Broil until top is golden.

SERVES 4.

Lemon verbena rice pudding

INGREDIENTS

3/4 cup (110 g) rice

1 cup (250 ml) lemon verbena leaves, loosely filled

1 cup (250 ml) milk

1/2 cup (125 ml) sugar

3 eggs

CARAMEL

1 cup (250 ml) sugar

1 tbsp. (15 ml) water

1 tbsp. (15 ml) lemon juice

Preheat the oven to 375 °F (190°C).

Cook rice in 2 cups (500 ml) of boiling water for 10 minutes. It should stay firm. Drain.

In the meantime, simmer leaves in milk. Strain.

Combine cooked rice, milk, sugar and eggs, and mix well. Reserve.

To make caramel*, combine sugar, water and lemon juice in a small saucepan and cook over medium heat without stirring, until the syrup turns golden. Pour into a baking or soufflé dish — ceramic or corning ware but not metal — and twirl to coat all sides. Handle the caramel with extra care, as it is very hot.

Pour rice mixture into the dish, set in a pan with 1 inch (2 cm) of water and bake for 30 minutes or until the center is firm to the touch. Cool before unmolding.

SERVES 6-8.

Caramel can also be made in the microwave oven. Combine all ingredients in an ovenproof dish and microwave at maximum for 6-8 minutes. Keep a close eye on it, and stop cooking when caramel is golden.

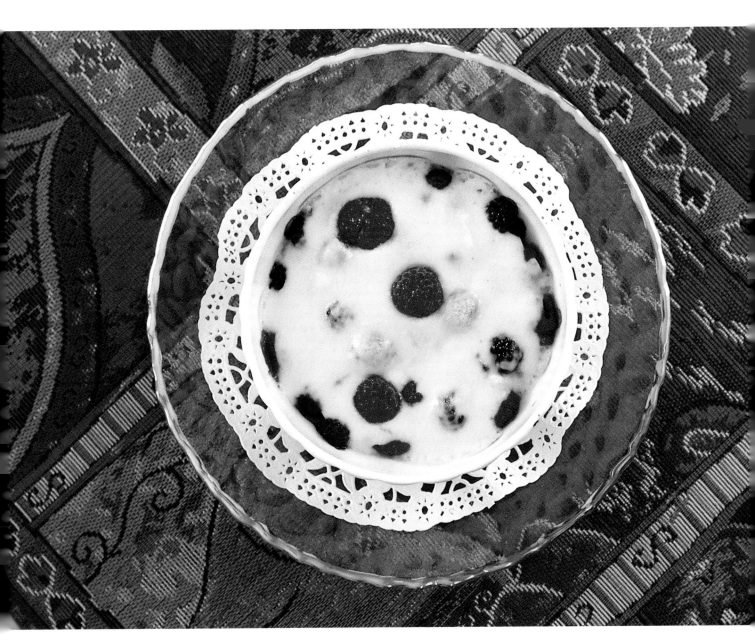

Berries au gratin

Quick apple tart with lemon basil

Wild apple trees abound in my area. Their fruit is deep red, pink or yellow, sometimes round, sometimes egg-shaped. Their flesh is crisp and bursting with flavors reminiscent of peach or pear. Marvellous!

I use them mostly for applesauce. As they are not treated with pesticides, I cook the fruit whole then remove skin and seeds by straining the pulp through a sieve. The resulting applesauce is smooth and silky. It is then flavored with flowers or herbs: beebalm, tarragon or lemon basil (my favorite).

I also cook sliced apples in butter until soft and serve them in a filo shell. Here's how.

INGREDIENTS

2 tbsp. (30 ml) butter

6 cups (1.5 liter) apples, peeled and sliced

1/2 cup (125 ml) sugar (or more)

1/4 cup (65 ml) lemon basil, chopped

4 sheets filo pastry

Melted butter + sugar

1/4 cup (65 ml) slivered almonds, roasted

Melt butter in a non-stick pan and cook apples over medium heat 3-4 minutes, stirring gently. Sprinkle with sugar to taste and cook until apples are soft but not falling apart. Add lemon basil, stir and reserve.

Preheat the oven to 400 °F (200 °C).

Spread one sheet of filo, brush with melted unsalted butter, sprinkle with sugar. Repeat until you have three layers. Transfer to a deep pie pan. Spoon apples in its center, sprinkle with almonds and bake for 15 minutes until golden. Serve warm.

SERVES 4-6.

Chocolate, mint and raspberry clafoutis

INGREDIENTS

3 cups (750 ml) fresh or frozen raspberries

1/2 (125 ml) cup flour

1 tsp. (5 ml) baking powder

1 tsp. (5 ml) baking soda

1/4 cup (65 ml) powdered cocoa

Pinch of salt

2 eggs, separated

1/4 cup (65 ml) soft butter

1/2 cup (125 ml) sugar

1 oz (60 g/2 squares) semi-sweet chocolate

1 tbsp. (15 ml) mint leaves, chopped

1/4 cup (65 ml) buttermilk or plain yogurt

Preheat the oven to 375 °F (190°C).

Butter a 9 x 12-inch (20 x 30 cm) oblong baking dish, sprinkle bottom with sugar and spread with fruit.

Combine dry ingredients. Beat together egg yolks and sugar until creamy and light in color. Melt chocolate squares and add to egg mixture with mint leaves. Beat in dry ingredients, alternating with buttermilk. Beat egg whites until stiff and fold into the chocolate mixture.

Spoon over fruit, level top with a spatula and bake 40 to 45 minutes, or until the center is firm.

Serve warm or cold with heavy cream or sweet scented custard (page 104).

SERVES 6-8.

Tip: No need to defrost frozen berries.

Crabapple-lavender jelly

Pure apple and crabapple juices make the best herb jellies. The high concentration of pectin sets the jelly in minutes — so fast that one has to monitor the process carefully — and their bland taste does not interfere with flavoring herbs.

INGREDIENTS

4 lb (2 kg) crabapples

1 cup (250 ml) water

2 1/2 cups (625 ml) sugar

2 tbsp. (30 ml) fresh lavender flowers

In a large pot, cook apples — no need to peel and core — with water until tender, about 20 minutes (2 minutes in a pressure cooker).

Pour fruit and juice in a jelly bag or a colander lined with cheesecloth (I use an old pillow case) and strain overnight. Do not squeeze the bag for the jelly will not be clear.

Measure juice and add enough water to make 3 cups (750 ml).

Combine juice and sugar, bring slowly to a boil, stirring constantly. Add lavender flowers and boil 5 to 8 minutes, until jelly point (see tip).

Ladle into hot, sterilized jars. Seal.

MAKES ABOUT 3 X 1 CUP (250 ML) JARS.

Tip: To determine when the jelly is about to set, you can use a candy thermometer, but it is not always accurate. You can also spoon a few drops onto a chilled plate. The jelly will cool on contact. If a "skin" forms on the surface and the jelly feels springy to the touch, it is ready. You can also mix 1 tsp. (5 ml) of fondue alcohol with 1 tsp. (1 ml) of jelly. It will clump when ready.

Variation:
ROSEMARY JELLY
Add 1/4 cup (65 ml) balsamic or apple cider vinegar and replace lavender with 6 rosemary sprigs. Use rosemary jelly to flavor meat sauces.

Lemonades

Mint, lemon balm, lemon verbena, scented geranium, lemon basil and even nasturtium leaves make wonderfully refreshing lemonades.

Just pour hot — but not boiling — water over a handful of leaves, steep 10 minutes and strain.

Add sugar to taste, and lemon or lime slices. Chill before serving.

Nasturtium and scented geranium lemonades are done in a blender. Combine 1 cup (250 ml) leaves and 3 cups (750 ml) water and process a few seconds at high speed. Strain, add sugar to taste, lemon slices and chill before serving.

Herbal teas

Herbal teas made from mint, lemon balm, lemon basil, cinnamon basil and lemon verbena help the digestive system. I often make a blend of these herbs to serve after a heavy meal.

Camomile is not my "cup of tea". I prefer ox-eye daisy, feverfew and yarrow.

And I mustn't forget stinging nettle, though it is not an herb. The tea made from this menacing-looking plant is rich in minerals. I drink a cup every morning for 10 days in the spring to give my winter-weary body a boost.

Pick young tender nettle shoots in spring when they are about 6 inches (15 cm) high. Wear gloves and a long sleeved shirt as the tiny hairs on the plant produce an intense, stinging pain, followed by redness and skin irritation. Dry on a fine mesh. Use about 2 tbsp. (30 ml) dried crushed leaves for 1 cup (250 ml) of water.

Index

WEIGHTS AND MEASURES

Logically, dry ingredients — flour, sugar, even vegetables — should be measured by weight, either in grams or ounces. But not everyone has a kitchen scale. Liquids should be measured by volume (ml, fluid ounces). How complicated! It's so much easier to use cups and spoons.

Bearing that in mind, I have marked all measures by volume, except in some instances for meat or cheese, when it is handy to know the weight for the sake of purchasing.

Here is the conversion chart, with figures rounded up or down for easier measuring.

1 tsp.	5 ml	
1 tbsp.	15 ml	
1 cup	250 ml	8 fluid ounces
4 cups	1 liter	1 quart
1 gallon	4 liters	4 quarts

National Library of Canada cataloguing in publication

Gardon, Anne

The gourmet's garden : cooking with edible flowers, herbs and berries

Translation of : Le gourmet au jardin.

Includes index.

ISBN 2-89455-135-5

1. Cookery (Flowers). 2. Cookery (Herbs). 3. Cookery (Fruit). I. Title.

TX814.5.F5G3713 2003   641.6'59   C2003-940522-2

The Publisher gratefully acknowledges the assistance of the Province of Québec, through the SODEC (Société de développement des entreprises culturelles) and the support of the Government of Canada, through the Book Publishing Industry Development Program.

Gouvernement du Québec - Programme de crédit d'impôt pour l'édition de livres - Gestion SODEC

© Guy Saint-Jean Éditeur Inc. 2000

© photographs Anne Gardon 2000

© For this edition in English, Guy Saint-Jean Éditeur inc. 2003

Editing: Alison Lee Strayer

Graphic Design: Christiane Séguin

Legal Deposit second quarter 2003

Bibliothèque nationale du Québec and the National Library of Canada

ISBN 2-89455-135-5

All rights reserved. The use of any of this publication, reproduced, transmitted in any form or by any means, electronic, mechanical, photocopying, recording or otherwise, or stored in a retrieval system, without the prior consent of the publisher is forbidden.

Green Frog Publishing is an imprint of Guy Saint-Jean Éditeur inc.

3154, boul. Industriel, Laval (Québec) Canada H7L 4P7.

Tel. (450) 663-1777. Fax: (450) 663-6666.

E-Mail: saint-jean.editeur@qc.aira.com   Web: www.saint-jeanediteur.com

Printed and bound in Malaysia